Prepper's Survival Stockpile

Build a Nutritious Emergency Pantry with Shelf-Stable Survival Foods and Be Self-Sufficient When Push Comes to Shove

Kenneth Olsen

Table of Contents

Introduction……………………………………………………………………………………1

Chapter 1: What's in a Prepper's Pantry?……………………………………2

Water……………………………………………………………………………………2

Food………………………………………………………………………………………2

Foods to stockpile……………………………………………………………………3

How much food do I need to stockpile?……………………………………5

What if I or my family have dietary restrictions?……………………………7

You have the list, now it's time to stockpile……………………………………8

Chapter 2: Budgeting, Shopping, and Finding Space……………………9

How to budget…………………………………………………………………………9

Where to shop………………………………………………………………………10

How to save money…………………………………………………………………11

Finding space in your home…………………………………………………13

Unique storage ideas…………………………………………………………14

What to know about food storage locations…………………………………15

Chapter 3: Maintaining and Rotating the Pantry……………………………17

How long should you keep food?……………………………………………17

Rotating your stockpile……………………………………………………………21

Tracking the pantry…………………………………………………………………21

Chapter 4: Storing Food..**23**

Storing water...23

Supplies for water storage and treatment...............................24

Storing food...26

Chapter 5: Preserving Food...**29**

Canning...29

Dehydrating...30

Freeze-drying..31

Smoking..31

Chapter 6: Cooking Under Crisis...**33**

First things first: do you need to ration food?........................33

Cooking methods and supplies...34

Cooking tips...36

Chapter 7: Food Stockpiling Do's and Don'ts.......................**38**

Do: Know your storage limits...38

Do: Practice cooking and using your stockpile items.............39

Do: Take the time now to get organized...................................39

Don't: Ration water or cut back dramatically on food............40

Don't: Depend on vitamins for nutrition..................................40

Don't: Stockpile only the bare essentials................................40

Epilogue..**42**

Introduction

Food and water - everyone needs them to survive. They are a basic human right. Unfortunately, there are times when a person's food security is threatened. It could be because of something personal like loss of income or something bigger like a destructive weather event. In a time of a pandemic, getting to the store and finding what you need could be challenging. There are countless scenarios when a stockpile of food and water would make life so much easier.

In this book, we're going to discuss all the basics of food stockpiling and storage. You'll learn what essentials you need and how to consider nutrition and special dietary concerns. To fit stockpiling into your budget, there are several ways to save money. Buying in bulk, using coupons, and keeping an eye on sales are all good. We'll also discuss where to find storage space in your home, how to store food properly so it stays good as long as possible, and how to preserve fresh foods.

The last chapters go over different cooking methods during an emergency when your options might be more limited. We'll also offer tips for success. Here's a tip to start you off: food and water are the most important things you can invest in. When you get into survival prepping, you'll see a lot of cool equipment and gear. Before you think about buying any of it, make sure you're on your way to a good food stockpile. These are the basics that will keep you and your family alive.

Chapter 1: What's in a Prepper's Pantry?

You know that water and food are the most important items you can stockpile, but what do you need exactly? In this chapter, we're going to go through a list of pantry items and discuss how much water and food you need to get.

Water

Water is the *first* thing you should think about when starting to prep for longer periods. Without water, humans can only survive a few days at the most. If your water gets shut off for some reason or it becomes unsafe to drink, would you have a backup? You first want to know how much water a person needs per day. Daily, experts recommend at least ½ gallon for each person. If you're sweating or sick, however, that amount goes up. To be absolutely safe, you should stock at least 1 gallon per person for every day you want to be prepared for.

If you have any pets, they'll also need water. Per day, dogs need around 1 ounce per pound of body weight. For every five pounds of body weight, cats need between 3 ½-4 ½-ounces.

You also need water for cooking and cleaning. In terms of how much, sources say about ¼ of a gallon per day for cooking and another ¼ for cleaning. Since this book is about food, we won't get into cleaning, but just know that a portion of your water should be reserved for that. There's a right way to store water, which we'll go over in a later chapter.

Food

When you look at a prepper's complete stockpile, what kinds of food can you expect to see? Nutrition is the #1 priority. Without good nutrition, your health will fail. You'll be more fatigued and vulnerable to sickness. Depending on the type of emergency that's going on, addressing the consequences of poor nutrition might not be easy. The best thing to do is to prevent these problems in the first place by eating well.

Nutritional needs

Humans need a variety of nutrients to stay healthy. Besides water, we need proteins, carbs, fats, minerals, and vitamins. These all come from food. While the amount of calories needed varies from person to person, humans generally need around 1,800 calories per day. You'll see different numbers floating around. Age, weight, gender, level of physical activity, health conditions, and even the season affect macronutrient needs.

Foods to stockpile

When you're stockpiling food items, you want to get the most nutrition possible from all your choices. You do not want foods with empty calories during an emergency. That doesn't mean you can't buy *any* snacks or treats, but since space will most likely be an issue, you want the vast majority of your food stock to be nutrient-dense. Here's a sample list of the kinds of things you'll need:

- Canned vegetables
- Canned chicken
- Canned fish
- Canned beans

- Canned fruit
- Canned soups
- Dry rice
- Dry pasta
- Pasta sauce
- Dry oats
- Instant oats
- Canned milk
- Powdered milk
- Powdered eggs
- Canned butter
- Canned olive oil
- Coconut oil
- Peanut oil
- Vinegar
- Baking soda
- Baking powder
- Cornstarch
- Peanut butter
- High-protein energy bars
- Honey
- Sugar
- Salt
- Black pepper
- Ground spices
- Condiments
- Flour
- Pet food

Did you expect a much longer list? The list gets longer the more specific it is. These are just the general, bare-necessity categories of food you'll need. What you get depends on what you like to eat, your budget, your space, and how long you want to store the food. We'll talk about how long certain food lasts, proper storage, and how to preserve food in chapters 3 and 4.

Can I just get MREs?

Stocking your prepper pantry is overwhelming, especially at the beginning. You might be tempted to just get MREs in bulk. MREs are "meals ready to eat" or camping food. These are typically freeze-dried meals that are ready to go. They just need hot water and a few minutes. These have been designed for nutritional value as well as taste. You can be confident you're getting what you need.

The other benefit of MREs is that they're packaged for you. There's no need to worry about pests and bacteria getting into a sealed bag. The MREs are also designed for a long shelf-life, though that exact time varies by brand. The downside is that MREs are expensive compared to canned and dry staples. You also don't have control over what the meals taste like, so if you don't like a flavor, you're out of luck.

What do I recommend?

Considering all your food options, I always lean toward variety. Go ahead and get the energy bars, instant oatmeals, etc., but don't depend on them. I also think MREs are a great idea, but again, in moderation. The majority of your food stockpile should be canned and dry staples. There's extra work when it comes to storage, but stockpiling this type of food factors in both nutrition and budget.

How much food do I need to stockpile?

You know what categories of food you need, but how much do you need to get? It depends on how far ahead you want to prepare for and how many people are in your family. FEMA recommends keeping a 3-day supply on hand at all times, but most prepper's want to plan for longer.

Meal planning for breakfasts, lunches, and dinners is the best way to calculate how much you need. For our example, let's start with one recipe per meal. You'll need more recipes so you don't lose your mind eating the same things every day, but for now, let's start simple. Here's our sample meal plan:

Meal	Dish	Ingredients
Breakfast	Oatmeal	Oats, water, nuts, brown sugar
Lunch	Chicken, rice, and beans	Canned chicken, water, rice, beans, spices
Dinner	Tuna Casserole	Canned tuna, cream of mushroom soup, macaroni noodles, water, peas, salt, and pepper

Write down the amounts you'll need for the proper amount of servings per recipe. For a family of four, that's about:

Oatmeal:

4 cups water	2 cups dry oats	2 tablespoons brown sugar	1 cup nuts

Chicken, rice, and beans:

4 cups water	2 cups uncooked rice	Two 12.5-ounce cans of chicken	One 15-ounce can of beans
Salt to taste	Pepper to taste	Other spices to taste	

Tuna casserole:

4 quarts of water	10-ounces macaroni noodles	Two 12.75-ounce cans of tuna	Two 12.75-ounce cans of cream of mushroom soup

1 ½ cups canned peas	Salt to taste	Black pepper to taste	

These are approximations because serving size will differ based on the person. Hunger will also increase or decrease depending on what physical activities you're doing.

Now, decide how many times a week you want this recipe lineup. Multiply the ingredient amounts by however many days you want to prep for. That's the amount you'll need to stockpile. To fill out the rest of the days, pick more recipes and repeat this process. Also think about how many snacks you think you'll need per day and get those, too. For stockpiling baking supplies, decide what you want to bake (like bread loaves) and how many times a week you'll be doing that. Figuring out these amounts takes a lot of work, but you only need to do it once. Write everything down and make sure you don't lose the information because you'll need to refer to it as you use and replenish the stockpile.

What if I or my family have dietary restrictions?

Food allergies and dietary restrictions are very common. If you and/or your family have any, you'll need to factor those into your prepping. Prepping is not one-size-fits-all. If you just stockpile from a list someone else wrote, you'll end up with food that could make someone sick or - at the very worst - kill them. You need to customize your prepping based on your needs. Even if someone has a mild allergy or sensitivity, don't plan on feeding them anything that will aggravate it. During an emergency, you want everyone to feel their best.

Common food issues include allergies, which vary in severity, as well as dairy intolerance and celiac disease. If someone is on a specialized diet or medication for high blood pressure or diabetes, it's also important to prep accordingly. People also may not eat certain foods for moral or religious reasons. While not health-related, you will still want to consider this when prepping. If you are the person on this type of diet, you may decide that during an emergency you're willing to adjust. If it's someone in your family, ask them what they are planning to do. With all the variety out there in the survival foods market, you can pretty easily accommodate any diet if you want to.

You have the list, now it's time to stockpile

As soon as you know how much drinking water you'll need and you have a few recipes and amounts written down, it's time to shop. In the next chapter, we'll go over budgeting concerns, where and how to shop, and how to find space for your stockpile.

Chapter 2: Budgeting, Shopping, and Finding Space

Prepping is not easy. It's an investment of emotional energy, mental energy, time, and yes, money. In this chapter, we're going to talk about how to budget for prepping, where to find your food, and how to find space in your home. Everyone's lifestyle is a little different, so take what you learn here and adjust it as needed.

How to budget

When you start out prepping, you'll write a list of things you believe are essential. First on the list: water and food. These are not negotiable. Also, unlike most other supplies, this is not an area where you want to try and scale back too much cost-wise. With water, you don't want to scale back at all. You should never plan on rationing water. If anything, you want to get more than you think you'll need.

You do have a little flexibility with things like brands (we'll talk about how to save money soon), but overall, the majority of your budget should be dedicated to food and water. Before you start spending big bucks on other supplies, make sure you have the food and water stockpile you need.

What if even the essentials break your budget? Life is expensive and you may not have a ton of money in the bank to set aside for prepping. The solution is to stockpile slowly. Meet the needs of a short-term emergency first where you can't get to the store for, say, two weeks. Focus on buying all the water you'll need and essential food items like rice, canned beans, and canned vegetables. You don't need to buy a year's worth of food and water in one swoop to be a good prepper. Even getting just one thing from your stockpile list each time you go to the store is great.

Where to shop

Your budget and how you shop are closely linked. Being smart about how you shop can save you money. One popular way is buying in bulk if your budget allows for it. While you need a bigger chunk of money upfront, you end up saving money on the amount of food you get. There are several places where it's easy to buy in bulk:

Costco/Sam's Club

These are very well-known stores that sell in large amounts. You do need to pay for a membership, but you can save a lot of money on food. You also get access to some surprising benefits like lower gas prices, discounts on pharmacy prescriptions, car part discounts, and so on.

Online

If you're a big online shopper, you'll love that you can get a food stockpile entirely on the web if you want. Amazon is a very popular site, especially if you have a Prime account because the shipping is free. There's also Boxed, which offers lower prices than even Amazon on some items. Membership is free.

Restaurant supply stores

Restaurants have to get their food supplies from somewhere and most aren't going to the regular grocery store. Restaurant supply stores offer bulk items for a variety of eateries, so you can get essentials like flour, rice, and more for good prices. Keep in mind that not all these stores are open to the public.

Ethnic grocery stores

Grocery stores dedicated to specific ethnic cuisines (Asian, Mexican, Indian, etc.) often sell essentials like rice, beans, spices, and more in bulk. You can find more unique food items for your stockpile, too. Oftentimes, the same products would be considered "special" in a regular grocery store and most likely cost a lot more.

Survival food companies

Some companies sell food specifically designed for long-term storage. That includes freeze-dried meals and individual ingredients, like vegetables. Legacy Food Storage sells a huge variety of freeze-dried food with a shelf life of up to 25 years. Choose from just about any size and food type. Mountain House is another popular brand. Buckets are sold in 29-32 serving sizes. These commercial survival brands can be pricey, but they do make it easy to stock up on nutrient-dense meals and ingredients that last a long time.

How to save money

You don't want to build a stockpile that's too small, but big ones can be expensive. How do you save money on the items you need? There are four methods:

Generic brands

One of the easiest ways to save a little money is to avoid big-name brands. These are nearly always more expensive than the generic versions. These are also known as private label or store brands. The concept of store brands started in the 1970s and continues to save consumers lots of money each year. These brands are growing as well, so odds are, you can find just about any item you want. Taste and nutritional content may vary a bit, so try it before committing it to your stockpile.

Coupons

Coupons have been around forever and for good reason. Some people get really into couponing and save significantly, but you don't need to get intense to make it worthwhile. The amount you save may seem small per trip, but over time, it can add up. You can find coupons in a variety of places like websites, apps, and local newspapers. Grocery stores also send coupons through the mail. Brands sometimes offer deals on their websites. The key to being a good couponer is organization. As soon as you get a new coupon, look at the end date. Use the ones that expire earliest first. Some people put their coupons in a booklet, but whatever works for you is fine.

Sales

Grocery stores have sales all the time, so you always want to be on the lookout. That doesn't mean you buy anything that goes on sale because you can end up spending more than you want that way. The secret is to mainly buy items you already planned on buying for your stockpile. If there's a really good sale on an item you didn't think of - but it's something essential like a canned vegetable, meat, etc. - go ahead and get it. Less popular items frequently have significant sales, as well as items near their expiration date. With prepping, you obviously don't want to get something that's about to expire, so make sure that's not the reason something is cheap.

Receipt-scanning apps

There are lots of phone apps that give you points every time you scan a receipt. These points add up and can be used on gift cards for groceries, retail, and more. The nice thing about these apps is that you aren't limited to scanning grocery receipts. Many apps take receipts from gas stations, convenience stores, clothing stores, and so on. Some popular apps include ReceiptPal, Fetch, and Ibotta.

Finding space in your home

Where do you put all the food and water you stockpile? Most people don't have a lot of space where they can easily accumulate a year's worth or more of items. The answer is to find space wherever you can and spread things out. Here are some ideas:

Kitchen pantry

This is the most obvious place to keep your food stockpile. Set aside a section of this area for your stockpile items and another for your everyday food. You don't want to accidentally start chipping away at your stockpile without knowing it.

Broom closets

Put boxes of items like canned and dry goods in broom closets. If you use the broom closets for other more everyday items, just put them on top of the stockpile so you can easily access them.

Bedroom closets

Bedroom closets often have space on the floor. Take advantage and store some of your stockpile there.

Basement

If your home has a basement, it's usually a great place for food items because it's cool and dark. Make sure dampness isn't an issue before moving your stockpile there.

Garage

A well-organized garage is another popular place for food and water. Just make sure you aren't storing your food near gasoline. Before moving your items there, think about how hot or cold the garage gets since garages aren't always well-insulated. If the temperature shifts too much, it isn't the best place for food.

Attic

If your house has an attic, it could work for storing some food items. Attics can get very hot or cold depending on the time of year, so it shouldn't be your first choice for a stockpile location. If you do want to use your attic, you can improve it slightly by making sure it's insulated. Installing a thermostatic heater and air conditioning to fight against temperature changes is also a good idea. All food should be properly sealed in Mylar bags and buckets. My recommendation is to use attic space for non-food prepping supplies.

Laundry room

A laundry room seems like a decent place to keep a food stockpile. However, that area is often humid, so it's not great for long-term storage. If you keep your food well-sealed in Mylar bags and food buckets, it should be all right as long as you're rotating the food. We'll talk about rotation and why it's a good idea in a later chapter.

Outdoor sheds/buildings

If you have a shed or other outdoor buildings on your property, it can work for food storage. Like garages, a shed is more vulnerable to extreme temperature changes. It can easily get too hot or too cold for your items. Before stockpiling there, you'll need to make some adjustments to make it work. Proper insulation, airflow, a thermostat, and more are important.

Unique storage ideas

You'll most likely find yourself running out of space as you build up your stockpile. You might also live in a small place where it's hard to find storage even when you're just starting. Here are some more unique storage ideas:

Under beds and furniture

Most people don't think about these areas as real storage potential. Depending on how tall the furniture is, you may have to get creative about what fits. Cans turned on their side will probably work. Be sure to clean thoroughly before moving your stockpile under there.

Shelving

Even in the smallest places, you can use the walls to your advantage. Installing some good shelving in a few rooms gives you more options for canned goods. You can also put up shelves in your closets and on the backs of doors. Make sure the shelves are strong enough to hold the weight of your items.

Decorative storage bins

Most people want to keep their stockpile out of sight, which makes sense. However, in small spaces, there just aren't that many options. That's why decorative storage bins are so convenient because they let you keep your stockpile out in the open, but not obvious. These bins can go in guest rooms, bedrooms, and even the living room. No one needs to know the bins are filled with canned and dry goods instead of board games or blankets.

What to know about food storage locations

No matter how much or how little space you have for food storage, be aware that you will most likely need to move your supplies around at certain times. The garage might work as a storage space for some months out of the year, but then it gets really hot in the summer. Same with the attic and an outdoor shed. While your supplies are in one area, think about where they could go next. Prepare ahead by building shelves, getting storage bins, and so on. Reorganize your other supplies - ones that aren't affected by temperatures - and make room for water and food.

As always, staying organized is important. You don't want to forget where you've put some food supplies and then discover them later in a sorry state. If you have food in areas that become unsuitable based on the season, monitor the temperature and humidity level so you know when to move them. Don't be tempted to get lazy when it comes to proper storage locations. It takes time and energy to get it right, but if you don't think about it, you'll end up losing supplies and that's a waste of time, energy, and money.

Chapter 3: Maintaining and Rotating the Pantry

Building a stockpile doesn't consist of just buying a bunch of stuff, putting it somewhere, and never touching it again. A good prepper knows the importance of maintaining and rotating their supplies. This includes staying organized with a list of expiration dates, using food as it gets closer to that date, and replacing it. In this chapter, we'll discuss how long certain foods are meant to last and the benefits of rotation.

How long should you keep food?

While you can get food that's meant to last 25 years, most of your stockpile will likely consist of canned and dry goods that don't last that long. If you're just buying food and sticking it in your pantry, here's how long you can expect stuff to last:

Note: In general, these lengths of time represent good storage conditions - cool, dark, and dry - with no extra work. We'll talk about how to get more years out of your food in the next chapter.

Water

Water doesn't expire, so it's the only supply you don't really need to worry about if the water is properly sealed and stored.

Canned food (fruit, vegetables, beans, meat)

Low-acid foods and canned meats usually last 2-5 years. Acidic foods expire sooner than other types of canned goods. These last 12-18 months. Should you pay attention to the package dates? With canned (and dry) food, you'll often see a few types of dates. There is a "best by" and "use by." If a can is past its "best by" date, it's still safe to eat. It just means that its nutritional content will go down as time passes. Even "use by" canned foods can usually be eaten a bit after their date.

Canned soups

In general, the same rules for canned fruit/vegetables/beans apply to canned soups. Plan on keeping these for 2-5 years at max.

Rice

Rice lasts a long time, so it's an ideal stockpile item. Uncooked white rice, wild rice, jasmine, Arborio, and basmati rice last for years. You don't really need to worry about expiration dates in terms of safety. The nutritional value does go down over time, so write down the "best by" date. Regardless of its age, if the rice looks normal and is completely dry, it's safe for consumption.

Brown rice, however, doesn't last long before it goes rancid. That's because it has more oil in it. In the pantry, it lasts 3-6 months. To extend its life, put it in the fridge (6-12 months) or freezer (12-18 months).

Pasta

Like rice, dry pasta lasts a long time. It can be eaten 1-2 years past its expiration date. If it looks dry, looks normal, and smells normal, it's safe to eat. It won't contain the same amount of nutrients, though.

Dried beans

Dried beans last for years when stored properly. Nutritionally, they do start to lose nutrients 2-3 years after their "best by" date. Dried beans will be safe to eat as long as you don't notice any bugs, mold, or odd smells.

Jarred sauce

Unopened, a jar of tomato/marinara sauce is at its best for 18-24 months. It will be safe to eat for around a year afterward. Always make sure it looks and smells normal before eating.

Oats

Stored in their original container, rolled oats keep all their nutrients for 18-24 months. They'll be safe for longer after that. As long as the oats are dry, you don't see any mold, and they smell normal, they're most likely safe.

Flour, baking soda, and baking powder

Unopened all-purpose flour stays fresh for 6-8 months. You can keep it at its best for up to a year in the fridge or for 2 years in the freezer. You'll know flour has gone bad when it smells rancid, sour, and musty. If you see any bugs or other contaminants in it, throw it out.

Baking soda and baking powder don't spoil, but they start to lose their effectiveness after their package date. Like flour, they can also become contaminated, so keep their lids sealed. They're at their best for about a year.

Canned milk

Unopened evaporated milk is at its best for about 6-12 months. It shouldn't be frozen. Condensed milk usually has a "best by" date of about 18-24 months, but it's safe for a long time afterward if it's stored properly. Canned coconut milk's shelf life is between 2-5 years. Coconut milk in a carton, unopened, should last 3-

4 weeks after its package date. No matter what type of milk you're using, signs of spoilage include an odd color, smell, and/or flavor.

Honey

Honey is one of the few foods that last forever. As long as it's protected from outside contaminants and kept away from direct sunlight, it will be safe to eat for the indefinite future. Over time, it can crystallize, but it's still safe.

Peanut butter

Peanut butter contains lots of oil which eventually goes rancid. Unopened peanut butter will be okay for about one year past its expiration date. Keeping it in the fridge or pantry doesn't seem to make a difference. Once regular peanut butter is open, it lasts for 3-4 months in the pantry and 6-8 months in the fridge. Keep in mind that the timeline doesn't include natural peanut butter, which goes bad quickly in only 2-3 months. I don't recommend natural peanut butter for stockpiling for this reason.

Sugar, salt, and dried spices

Sugar, salt, and dried spices don't go bad in the traditional sense. The quality just goes down. Spices will start losing their flavor and nutrition after 3-4 years of storage.

Cooking oils

Oils go rancid. Some last longer than others. Canned olive oil will last longer than regular olive oil. Unopened sunflower seed oil and coconut oil last around 2 years while unopened peanut oil lasts 3 years. You can extend the life of most oils by keeping them in the fridge.

Rotating your stockpile

Rotating your stockpile isn't difficult, but it does require good organizational skills. You want to eat the food that's closest or just past its package date and replace it. Why? Your stockpile will always be its best in terms of nutrition. While most foods technically last way past their "best by" date, they lose nutrients as time passes. You don't want to end up with a stockpile that offers no nutritional value. You also don't want a stockpile that's so old, you're not 100% sure something is safe to eat. Getting sick is the last thing you want during a crisis.

Digging into your stockpile regularly also allows you to catch any storage problems before they ruin all your supplies. This saves you money in the long run. You'll also get to eat some of the foods you don't normally use, so you can be sure you like them.

What about water? As you know, water doesn't expire, but if possible, you always want your water to be fresh. Some prepper's recommend rotating your water supply every year or so. You can use it for drinking, washing, or cooking and then replace it. This also lets you check on your water to make sure you've been storing it properly. If you forget to rotate a supply, but you know it's sealed and safe, you don't have to stress about it too much. It is more about its freshness than anything else.

Tracking the pantry

The key to maintaining and rotating your pantry is staying organized. Keep a list of all your items and write down their package dates. Some prepper's write the package date in large letters directly on the item as well, so they don't need to refer to their master list every time. You can also set yourself reminders in a digital calendar, so you'll be notified when a date is coming up.

As soon as you use an item, write it on a list so you know you need to replace it. Do you need to replace it right away? You don't need to make a special trip to the store to get a single can of tomatoes, but don't wait too long. You want your stockpile as complete as possible at all times because you don't know when an emergency might arise.

Chapter 4: Storing Food

You have an idea about how long food lasts, but that represents certain storage conditions. All food, including canned food, needs to be stored properly or it won't last as long as it could. In this chapter, we're going to discuss how to store your stockpile so it lasts as long as possible. Let's start with your most important stockpile item: water.

Storing Water

All water should be stored in a cool, dark place. You want to keep it out of direct sunlight as this degrades the material. It should also be kept away from any chemicals or gasoline since those fumes can leach into your supply.

There are a few ways to store water. Just stockpiling bottled water you get at the store is the simplest method. You can rest assured that these bottles are food-grade, sealed, and safe to drink. They aren't ideal for long-term storage, though, as the plastic degrades over time.

Long-term storage

If you want to store a supply for a long time, you'll need a water storage container. These come in a bunch of sizes as small as 5 gallons. There are large

55-gallon ones, as well. The best size for your needs depends on how much space you're working with.

Step 1: The first step is to clean the container. Squirt in some dish soap and fill about a quarter of the way with warm water. Shake the container or roll it around. Rinse well. If you don't want to use soap, just hot water will work, too. If you're working with a big container, a drinking water hose is the way to go. A regular garden hose may contain contaminants that flush into your containers.

Step 2: Once you've filled your containers with water, you can add a water treatment solution. Water doesn't expire or "go bad," but bacteria can grow inside. If you're using a drinking water hose or water from the tap, it's already been treated, so you're most likely fine. If you do choose to use a preserver, you can find a handful of brands on websites like Amazon. Always follow the instructions carefully for volume per gallon of water.

Step 3: The last step is to seal the containers. This is very important because you don't want anything nasty getting in your fresh water. When it's time to drink your water and you're worried it wasn't sealed properly, you can boil it or add a water treatment pill. Know that water that's been stored for a while will have a flat taste, but that doesn't mean it's been contaminated.

Supplies for water storage and treatment

Besides regular water containers, here's a list of what you'll need for storing water or making water safe to drink:

A WaterBob - This container is best for short-term water emergencies. It's a big plastic bladder you put in the bathtub and fill with water. You would use this in situations when you anticipate a storm or other events that will cut off the running water. Put it in the tub and fill with water before that happens. The WaterBob is made with food-grade plastic and can hold up to 100 gallons.

Water filters - In situations where you do have access to water, but it's contaminated, you'll want filters in addition to your water stockpile. There are all kinds of choices, including pitcher-style filters and ones that attach to your sink. When making your selection, think about how much work the filter requires, how much water it's designed to filter, its durability, and so on. For on-the-go water filtering, get some pocket filters like the LifeStraw. These are ideal for camping and bugging out.

Water treatment pills - You'll want these to add to your water when you suspect it's contaminated. Aquatabs is a very well-known brand, but there are lots of options out there. Pill size and number of pills varies depending on how much water you want to treat, so always follow the directions.

Bleach - I like water treatment pills better than bleach, but unscented chlorine bleach can purify water. You want to make sure the bleach is meant for sanitization and disinfection. For every quart of water, you'll need two drops of bleach. Add four if the water looks cloudy. Mix and let the water rest for a half-hour. The water should have a slight bleach smell after that time, but if not, add another 2-4 drops and wait 15 minutes.

Rain harvesting gear - If you want to be a prepper who thinks of everything, you'll want rain harvesting gear. Because water is essential to life and it shouldn't be rationed, even the biggest stockpile will eventually run out. Rain harvesting gear lets you collect rainwater in larger amounts, which you can then treat, drink, and store! Setting up the gear takes a bit of work at first, but it's worth it.

When in doubt, boil the water

Safe drinking water is your #1 priority as a prepper. If you're ever in doubt, I recommend boiling the water if possible. This lets you keep your other water treatment supplies for emergencies. Boiling for safety is simple. In a pot, bring the water to a rolling boil. That heat kills disease-causing bacteria and viruses. The CDC recommends boiling for a minute to be sure everything is dead. The one downside to boiling is that it doesn't remove chemical toxins.

Storing food

After water, storing your food properly is essential for long-term prepping. The process is a bit more complicated because unlike water, food does go bad. The goals with storage are to keep the food protected from contaminants and extend its shelf-life as long as possible. Here's what you want to do:

Canned food

Canned food is usually cheap and already sealed, so it's a popular item to stockpile. You do need to store it properly, though. The first thing to watch for is temperature extremes. The hotter a can gets, the more likely the food inside will go bad. Freezing can also cause problems. Store your cans in a cool, dark, and dry place. Between 50-70 degrees should be fine. As long as the can is undamaged, it's most likely safe to eat. If it's showing signs of rust or dents, throw it out. This damage means the food has probably been exposed to air and all kinds of bacteria, so don't risk it.

Dry goods

Dry goods are the other main staple of most stockpiles. This includes flour, rice, oats, pasta, and so on. With these foods, remember that oxygen and moisture are bad. Your mission is to keep the dry goods as sealed off from the elements as possible. You'll need four supplies for this purpose:

- Mylar bags

- Oxygen absorbers

- Heat sealer

- Food-grade buckets

Mylar bags

Whenever you buy a dry supply, you want to move it from its original container into a Mylar bag. These bags are made from a material called Mylar, which is flexible, light, and thin. At the same time, it's also very durable, so it's used for all kinds of things like solar filters and space blankets. It's also used to make food-grade bags that are tight and sealed off from the air outside. Mylar bags come in a variety of sizes and thicknesses. 1-gallon bags are good for food items like spices, baking powder, dried meat, and dried fruit. A 5-gallon bag works well for food you want to store in bulk, like flour and rice. The thickness matters because the thicker the bag, the better it is at keeping light out. The price does go up with the thickness, but don't get the cheapest one if you want to protect your food.

Oxygen absorbers

You want to pair your Mylar bags with oxygen absorbers. When sealed in a bag, these little packets of iron powder suck up the oxygen that causes food spoilage. Their purpose is to extend the shelf life of food much further than normal. Absorbers come in a variety of sizes and to make sure you aren't wasting them, you want to only use what you have to. They're in sizes 50-2000 cc. The size you need depends on the bag size. In general, you'll use 300-500cc per gallon of food.

Heat sealer

Once you have your food and oxygen absorbers in a Mylar bag, you need to seal it. In theory, you can use anything that generates heat, like a hair straightener or iron, but it's best to get a real Mylar bag sealer. These give you much better control over the heat because if it's too hot, it'll melt holes in your bag. Not hot enough and you won't get a good seal. When sealing, make sure the bag is flat. Check for any food debris or visible dust in the area before sealing.

Food buckets

In theory, you could just take your sealed bags of food and pile them up in your storage area, but they're still vulnerable. The best decision is to put them in food-grade buckets. It's an extra layer of protection that ensures your food lasts a long time. Like bags, buckets come in a handful of sizes. What works best for you depends on how much food you're storing and your space. If you have a 5-gallon bag of food, a 5-gallon bucket will work. You can also put multiple smaller bags in a big bucket if you want. Seal and label the buckets. Store in a cool, dry, and dark place away from chemicals or gasoline.

Chapter 5: Preserving Food

Storing canned and dry food is fairly simple, but what if you want to preserve your own food for your stockpile? This lets you buy more fresh things when they're cheaper. You can keep them tasty and safe for much longer. In this chapter, we'll go over the four main ways to do this: canning, dehydrating, freeze-drying, and smoking.

Canning

People have been canning food for centuries. You can preserve a wide variety of items such as fruits, vegetables, soups, jam, and more. People like canning because it lets them buy produce when it's cheap and save it for later. There's also the benefit of quality control. Canning is an investment (both money and time), but the knowledge is worth it. Here are the supplies you'll need:

- Quart and/or pint jars

- Lids and bands

- Jar lifter

- Jar funnel

- Canning salt

- Pressure canner

The pressure canner will cost the most, but it's necessary if you want to be sure your canned food is safe. A normal "water bath canner" is only good for fruit, so if you want to be able to can more, get the pressure canner.

You can find countless canning recipes online, but the process is generally the same. Take your fresh produce and wash it. Vegetables should be blanched. Boil them in water for a few minutes and then immediately move them to ice water to stop the cooking process. For soups, cook everything with hot water, tomatoes, or broth until boiling. Boil for five minutes and add salt. You want to stop cooking the soup before it's done because the canning process finishes it off. Certain soups, like any soups with dairy, can't be canned. With meat, you want to cook until tender. Cool and then remove the bones. Always follow a recipe's directions and make sure to adjust if necessary based on your jar size and altitude. Home-canned foods don't last as long as commercial cans, so plan on eating them within a year or so.

Dehydrating

Dehydration works on a variety of food, like fruits, vegetables, and meat. As the name suggests, the dehydration process involves removing moisture from the food. This helps it last longer because moisture is what allows bacteria to grow. You can dehydrate in the oven, but a real dehydrator machine is probably the best way to go. Machines cost between $60-$250 or so.

To prepare produce for dehydration, it should be washed, dried, and cut into slices. If the pieces are too large, it will take forever to dry out. You can dehydrate food with spices, so they taste more interesting. The dehydration process mellows out the flavor a bit and some nutrients are lost. You can find countless dehydration recipes online. Once you've dehydrated your food, store it in a sealed Mylar bag with oxygen absorbers.

Freeze-drying

Freeze-drying is not the same as dehydrating. Freeze-drying removes about 98% of the water content while dehydration removes 80%. This means freeze-dried food lasts longer. The process is different, too. Freeze-dried food is frozen below zero in a vacuum chamber. The temperature is slowly raised, so the moisture in the food moves from a frozen form to a vapor, leaving the food. In the past, you couldn't do freeze-drying at home. Now, Harvest Right sells an at-home freeze dryer. They are not cheap. A small one will cost you upwards of $2,100. It's definitely an investment, but commercial freeze-dried food is also expensive. Freeze-drying all your food will likely cost less than buying the same amount from a company.

Freeze-dried meat will have the longest shelf life of any meat in your stockpile. Sealed in its package, it can last up to 25 years. Once opened, you should eat it within the next few weeks.

Smoking

Humans have preserved meat for centuries using smoking. It's like dehydration in that the goal is to remove moisture, but smoking is done with wood chips for added flavor. Depending on the chips you use, the meat will have a different taste. The key is to smoke using indirect, low-temperature heat for a long time. This dehydrates the meat, making it less hospitable to bacteria.

Nowadays, smoking is mostly done just for flavor and not for food preservation, but it's still possible to use this method to extend meat's lifespan. Besides smoke, salt is important. It's either sprinkled on the meat or mixed with water as a brine. This salty mixture sits on the meat for a certain time before you rinse it off. This is known as "curing." There's a balance between using too little salt - which will shorten the meat's lifespan - and using too much - which results in an unpleasant flavor. Find a reliable recipe if you're new to curing. Depending on what you're cooking, curing may not be essential, but it can extend the life of smoked meat.

You'll need a smoker. There are a few types other than traditional wood smokers, such as gas smokers and electric smokers. If you're new to smoking, gas and electric are easier to learn, but they have some downsides. Gas smokers tend to produce food with less flavor, while electric smokers are pricey and they're useless if your power goes out. Wood chips are always a part of the process no matter what smoker type you get, so you'll also need wood. The type of wood you choose affects the flavor. Make sure the wood you're using has been approved for food or it could make your meat toxic.

Smoking times vary depending on the type of smoker. It usually takes hours because the temp needs to be low and slow. Once the meat is done, store properly. I recommend freezing the meat in Ziploc bags as this will extend its life to a year if it's also been cured. Smoked fish lasts 2-3 months.

Chapter 6: Cooking Under Crisis

When you're in an emergency, your cooking habits might change. Depending on the crisis, different problems could pop up. Maybe your power is out and you can't use your oven and stovetop. Maybe your trips to the grocery store are limited, so you're cooking through your stockpile and need to make every meal stretch as much as possible. In this chapter, we'll go through nutritional concerns you need to think about, emergency cooking equipment, and cooking tips.

First things first: do you need to ration food?

Depending on the kind of emergency you're dealing with, you may not need to ration food too much. If you're able to access groceries more easily, rationing won't be as much of a concern, but saving money might be. You want to use your stockpile efficiently.

The first thing you need to know is that you should not ration water. This is dangerous. Your normal food consumption can be cut down a bit if necessary, but it should be done safely. Food should not be rationed for children or pregnant women. In general, women (who aren't pregnant) need at least 1200 calories a day to maintain their weight while men need at least 1500 calories. If you're active, you'll need more. Stress can also amplify or repress your appetite, so how you feel isn't always a great guideline to follow during tough times. If you know stress tends to trigger overeating and you want to avoid that, you'll need to be more precise about servings.

Nutrition plays a big role, as well. Eating 1200 calories of only pasta is not going to do your body good compared to 1200 calories of pasta, canned meat, and vegetables. In addition to paying attention to calorie count, you want to watch your meal's variety.

Ideally, you want to design your meal plans before an emergency happens. This way, you don't need to worry about counting calories and nutrients while stressed. You can just follow your meal plans and recipes, knowing that each serving reflects at least the minimum nutritional and caloric content needed for health.

Cooking methods and supplies

Your normal cooking methods might not be an option during an emergency. If you can't use the microwave, oven, or stovetop, how do you prepare your food? There are a handful of choices:

Camping stove

There are tons of camping stoves out there that use a variety of energy sources. Most are reasonably affordable. Fuel sources include propane, butane, and even solar energy. Some types can be used safely indoors, but always check before beginning to cook. Charcoal should never be used indoors. Denatured alcohol stoves are safer indoors than propane or butane. There are also many sizes of camping stoves, which is great if you want a portable cooking source.

Outdoor grill

If you have an outdoor grill, you can rely on that to cook just about anything. Wrap meals in foil, put food directly on the grill, or use a cast-iron skillet. You can find countless recipes for basically any type of dish for the grill.

Indoor fireplace

If you have a wood-burning fireplace, you can use that to cook. There are grills you can use in the fireplace that make the process easier. Stockpile wood alongside your food supplies if you plan on using your fireplace.

MRE heater

If you want to save fuel and energy and you have MREs, you can just use an MRE heater for those dishes. These pouches are used by campers and servicemen. They are a combination of powdered food-grade iron, magnesium, salt, and water. When water is poured in the heater pad, it releases enough heat to warm up the MRE in about 12 minutes. These should be used in a well-ventilated area because even though they don't produce carbon monoxide, they can activate detectors. I haven't seen other cooking uses for MRE heaters except for hot drinks like instant coffee or cocoa.

Traditional wood stove

A wood stove isn't a common feature in most homes these days. If you have the money and space, getting one installed can set your mind at ease should the power go out. These stoves are also a heat source that is perfect for cold winters.

Outdoor fire pit

You can dig a fire pit or buy one that's above ground. There are also different types of fuel you can use, such as propane, natural gas, or wood. Ease of use and price vary depending on the fuel type and other features of the pit.

Cooking supplies

In addition to the normal pots and pans you most likely also have for cooking, you'll also need firestarters, fuel (wood, propane, butane, etc.), a few can openers, and a cast-iron skillet.

Cooking tips

You don't need to be a master chef to cook well during stressful times, but here are some tips that can help make the experience easier:

Don't use more water than you need

Depending on the emergency, you might want to conserve the water you use for cooking. Most people use too much water when they're boiling food like pasta and rice. You only need enough so the food is just submerged. You can also save water by preparing vegetables using the steam created by cooking potatoes, pasta, rice, etc. Just put a steamer basket on top of the boiling pot. Did you know that you can reuse pasta water? Instead of dumping it down the sink, save it and use it for cooking more pasta, rice, and bread. You can even use it to water plants. Throw out reused water that's become very cloudy.

Use spices

Don't be afraid to use spices in your cooking. Bland food is boring. Certain spices can even help make you feel fuller. Cayenne pepper contains capsaicin, an ingredient that's shown to boost your metabolism and suppress hunger. There's also evidence that ginger can help reduce appetite and stimulate the digestive system.

Reduce energy consumption with cold meals if possible

Not all your food needs to be cooked to make a good meal. Vegetables can be mixed for delicious and nutritious salads, while oats can soak overnight in water or milk. Serve canned fruit for dessert instead of baked goods. These cold meals are especially refreshing during the hot summer months.

Learn how to use your equipment and practice meals

The best cooking tip I can offer is to learn how to use your equipment and make the meals you would serve during an emergency. You can figure out if you like a recipe or adjust it based on your family's tastes. Trying out the equipment now also lets you avoid mistakes during an actual emergency and decide if a particular method works for you. Like rotating your stockpile, using your gear and practicing recipes is an important part of fully preparing for any kind of crisis.

Chapter 7: Food Stockpiling Do's and Don'ts

Building an emergency pantry can be overwhelming, especially if you're new to prepping. You learned a lot in the last six chapters. In this final chapter, let's go over some tips that can help you succeed. As you build up your pantry, remember these do's and don'ts.

Do: Know your storage limits

One of the first things you should do when getting ready to stockpile is think about your space. Where will all your food go? There are certain areas that experts don't recommend for food (like under your sink, over the oven, in the laundry room, etc.), so these should be crossed off your list for now. Check out your closets, bedrooms, basement, and anywhere else you believe will work. Some reorganization may need to be done to maximize these areas. Consider building shelving and getting storage bins. You don't need to have all the areas primed and ready to go before you start stockpiling, but knowing where you can make more space is always good.

Knowing your storage limits can also help you know what items to prioritize. If you don't have a ton of space, you'll want to focus on items that ensure your survival, like water, canned vegetables, protein sources, and so on. Filling your limited storage space with tons of energy bars and bags of flour won't help you in an emergency. Depending on how limited your space is right now, your pantry may not look as varied as you would like it. However, you can be confident you at least have enough water and essential nutrients.

Do: Practice cooking and using your stockpile items

Prepping is as much about the skills and knowledge you accumulate as the physical items. This is true whether it's knowing how to use medical supplies or how to start a fire. When it comes to food stockpiling, your skill-building consists of cooking meals. As foods draw close to the end of their peak nutritional value, you'll want to use them and replace them with fresh food. Make the recipes you would prepare during a time of crisis so you can experiment with flavorings. You can also see how many servings the recipes actually make and if it's enough. If you've stockpiled cooking equipment like camping stoves or MRE heaters, practice using those, too. You'll get comfortable with them so that when a time comes when you need to use them, you'll be fine.

Do: Take the time now to get organized

There's a lot of list-writing in food stockpiling. You want a list of types of food you'll need and the amounts. You'll also have meal plans and a list of package dates. Getting organized can take a lot of work, but it is more than worth it later on. By taking the time and energy now, you're saving yourself a lot of time and energy later. You'll also end up saving money because if you don't know when your food expires, you won't be able to gradually rotate and replace them properly. Instead, you'll end up with large batches of food that aren't great and you'll need to spend a larger amount of money to replace everything.

Good organization also includes committing to proper storage conditions. This ensures your food lasts as long as possible, so you aren't constantly rotating and replacing things. When you take the time to carefully store essential food and water supplies, you can sleep easy at night knowing everything is sealed and protected.

Don't: Ration water or cut back dramatically on food

During a crisis, you never want to ration your drinking water. During stockpiling, if you aren't sure you have enough, get more. If you have a limited storage space, water should be your top priority. Not getting enough water can have serious health consequences. At the very least, you'll feel fatigued and ill. The added stress of living through an emergency won't help, either. Keep in mind that if you're physically active, sick, or sweaty, you'll need more water than usual.

In this same vein, you want to be careful about rationing food. There is more flexibility here than with water, but your body still needs a minimum amount of nutrients to function properly. Don't slash your normal caloric intake per day during a crisis just so you can save on storage space. Nutrition is more important. Talk to your doctor about your specific nutritional needs and come up with recipes that meet a basic requirement for good health.

Don't: Depend on vitamins for nutrition

Speaking of nutrition, you shouldn't neglect to get healthy food and try to fill in the gaps with bottled vitamins. Vitamins are best provided to the body through food. The vitamin industry is also rife with low-quality brands, so it's easy to get something that won't do you much good. This doesn't mean you can't get *any* vitamins - they're a good idea if your storage space is really limited and you have specific needs - but you certainly shouldn't depend on them. Focus on getting nutritionally-dense foods first. Afterward, if you have space or are concerned about getting enough nutrients, go ahead and get high-quality vitamins.

Don't: Stockpile only the bare essentials

In theory, people can survive on very little. Rice and beans are a complete protein, so with plenty of water, you could survive for quite a while. However, you won't feel very well. Health problems will pop up. When stockpiling, balance the need for good nutrition with foods that help with your mental health. This could mean stockpiling your favorite tea or freeze-dried desserts in addition to the staples necessary for life. Emergencies can take a toll on your emotional well-being and something as simple as a cup of coffee could help you adjust. You do want to prioritize the essentials first, but don't stop there. Your mind and heart will need feeding, just like your physical body.

Epilogue

There are countless blogs, books, and even TV shows dedicated to survival prepping. Every prepper would say the most important thing you can focus on first is food and water. Without these, you won't survive very long. In this book, we explored what a prepper's pantry should look like, complete with water, canned goods, dry goods, and MREs. Foods high in nutrition and calories are very important. You can find food at any grocery store, as well as restaurant supply stores, survival food companies, and other places. Even people with tight budgets can prep by taking advantage of sales, coupons, and buying a few items at a time.

How you store your food is essential, as well, or it won't be good when it comes time to eat it. There are lots of places in your home that work, as well as places that aren't quite as ideal. A mixture of proper storage conditions thanks to Mylar bags, food storage bins, and preservation all ensure long shelf lives.

To maintain your pantry's freshness, a rotation system is best. Keep a list of package dates and as the dates come up, use the food and replace it. This allows you to create emergency meals and use cooking equipment like camping stoves. Prepping is all about building skills and knowledge alongside supplies. That applies to your food stockpile, too.

Whether your goal is two weeks' worth of supplies or a stockpile that lasts for years, I hope this book provided a useful roadmap. Good organization is key to your success. Get the layout of your home to find storage space, write lists, and keep digging into your supplies when necessary.

54970670R00028